The Miracle of You

Cleere Cherry Reaves

Illustrated by Alejandra Barajas

Tommy NELSON

An Imprint of Thomas Nelson

The Miracle of You

© 2023 Cleerely Stated, LLC

Tommy Nelson, PO Box 141000, Nashville, TN 37214

Published in Nashville, Tennessee, by Tommy Nelson. Tommy Nelson is an imprint of Thomas Nelson. Thomas Nelson is a registered trademark of HarperCollins Christian Publishing, Inc.

Published in association with the literary agency of Wolgemuth & Associates.

Tommy Nelson titles may be purchased in bulk for educational, business, fund-raising, or sales promotional use. For information, please email SpecialMarkets@ThomasNelson.com.

Scripture quotations are taken from the Holy Bible, New Living Translation. Copyright © 1996, 2004, 2015 by Tyndale House Foundation. Used by permission of Tyndale House Ministries, Carol Stream, Illinois 60188. All rights reserved.

ISBN 978-1-4002-4214-6 (eBook)
ISBN 978-1-4002-4210-8 (HC)

Library of Congress Cataloging-in-Publication Data

Names: Reaves, Cleere Cherry, 1990- author. | Barajas, Alejandra, illustrator.
Title: The miracle of you / Cleere Cherry Reaves ; illustrated by Alejandra Barajas.
Description: Nashville, Tennessee, USA : Thomas Nelson, [2023] | Audience: Ages 4-8 | Summary: "A beautiful celebration of your child's uniqueness among all of God's creation, this colorful picture book by Cleere Cherry Reaves speaks the words on your heart about what a God-given miracle your little one will always be"-- Provided by publisher.
Identifiers: LCCN 2022043608 (print) | LCCN 2022043609 (ebook) | ISBN 9781400242108 (hc) | ISBN 9781400242146 (ebook)
Subjects: LCSH: God (Christianity)--Juvenile literature. | Miracles--Juvenile literature.
Classification: LCC BT107 .R438 2023 (print) | LCC BT107 (ebook) | DDC 231--dc23/eng/20230117
LC record available at https://lccn.loc.gov/2022043608
LC ebook record available at https://lccn.loc.gov/2022043609

Written by Cleere Cherry Reaves

Illustrated by Alejandra Barajas

Printed in the United States

23 24 25 26 27 PC 7 6 5 4 3 2

Mfr: Phoenix Color / Hagerstown, Maryland / March 2023 / PO #12201913

To my son, Sledge, my living miracle. I am so
honored to be your mama. Your story forever changed
everything about mine. May you never stop telling
others about the Miracle Worker, who gave you life.
—Mom

He will cover you with his feathers. He will
shelter you with his wings. His faithful
promises are your armor and protection.
—Psalm 91:4

For my mom and dad.
Thank you for always being with me.
—Alejandra

God's miracles are everywhere.
They're treasures, big and small.
And tiny things can sometimes
be the greatest of them all.

He crafted your sweet smile,
and He made your bright eyes too.

Can anything that God
has made compare to precious you?

What about the **oceans**?

They **stretch** as far as we can see, connecting all the continents and **everything** between.

What about the creatures swimming deep within the sea, all colors, shapes, and sizes—from the shark to manatee?

I'm amazed by every wondrous thing within the ocean blue, but nothing in the sea can match

the miracle of you.

What about the **airplanes** soaring high across the sky?

Their wings can split the clouds above. Oh, how they can **fly!**

What about big **Sailing ships** that leave the dock and shore, taking us to places that we've wanted to explore?

These creations can't compete
with what I know is true: the very best adventure is
the **miracle** of you.

What about the moon and stars and how they shine at night? Their glow reminds us to look up and always find the light.

What about the universe and galaxies inside?

The mysteries of outer space keep reaching far and wide.

The sparkles of the universe create the coolest views, but all the stars cannot outshine

the miracle of you.

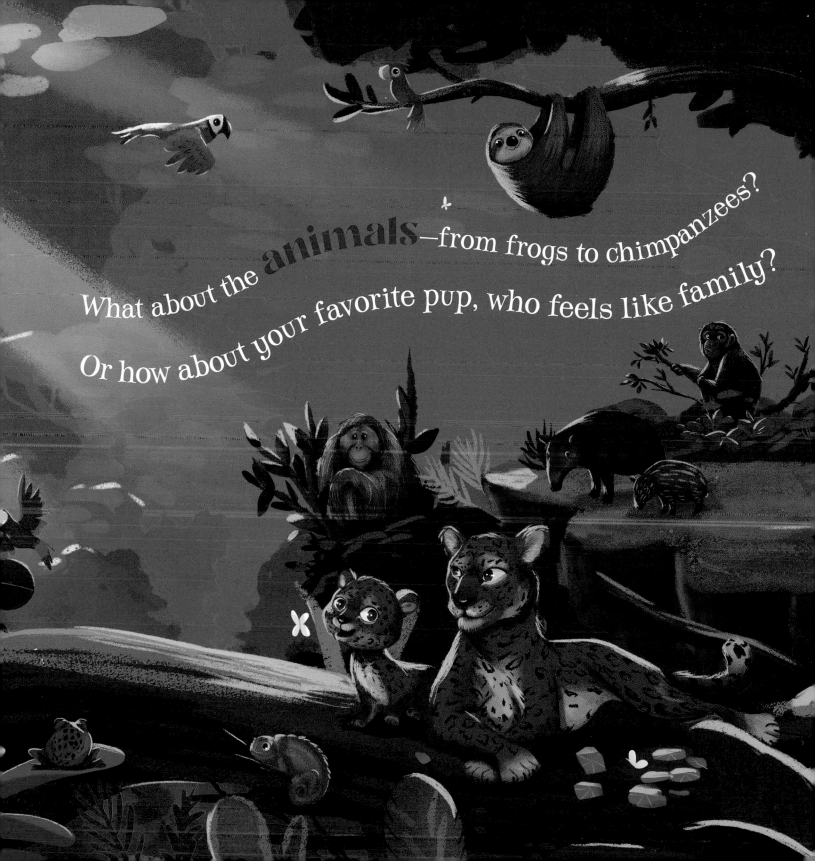

What about the **animals**—from frogs to chimpanzees?

Or how about your favorite pup, who feels like family?

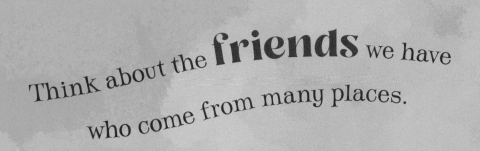

Think about the **friends** we have
who come from many places.

They show us that **God's love**
is found on lots of different faces!

But if I had to choose just one to give my lifetime to,

I'd always pick to spend it with

the miracle of you.

Nothing else in this **whole** earth or in the **sky** above could ever mean as much to me as **you,** my little love.

You're my favorite miracle.
I love you through and through.

No other treasure could compare to
the **miracle** of **you.**